SO YOU WANT TO BE A HOME INSPECTOR?

HERE'S HOW!

FOR BUYER, SELLER OR PROFESSIONAL

BY

Albert E. Wise II

WISE HOME INSPECTION SERVICE, INC.

Introduction

Let me first say how excited I am that you have picked up this book, the do-it-yourself book of home inspections. You are now well on your way to becoming a home inspector. With the help of this book, you will learn the ins and outs of inspecting a home. I have written it specifically for anyone who wants to become a home inspector or would just like to do his or her own inspection of a potential real estate property for purchase.

A little about myself: my background is in construction, plumbing, and heating. I was a licensed master plumber in Arkansas and Mississippi. I was also licensed as a general contractor and master plumber in Tennessee. I currently hold a master plumbing license in Florida. I became a home inspector in the early 1970s, before it was a popular business, and have trained other people to become home inspectors. Many of the real estate companies would ask me to check the plumbing and heating on homes that they were selling. This evolved into inspecting the entire home, which started my home inspecting business. At that time, home inspection classes were not available and there was not a way to learn the business.

Over the years, I have come across many home inspectors with no background in construction or any related trades and with no relevant experience. That is why I have written this book. That's not to say that you can't be a good home inspector if you don't have a background in construction, but it does help to have some. I have used the information provided in this book to train people to do home inspections. A high-quality inspection is important so that a buyer knows what he or she is purchasing and can determine what it will cost to make any needed repairs. This information will help a buyer decide whether to make an offer and how much to offer for a property. It will also help a seller to put his or her home in the best condition before placing the home on the market in order to receive a better price for the home.

This book lays out the necessary steps to become a superior home inspector. The most important thing is to not overlook anything; if someone were inspecting a home you were planning to purchase, you would want that inspector to leave no stone unturned in checking it for you.

The book also contains a report that you can use for your home inspections. It is a short version of a home inspection report, which I think is the best one to use because it gets right to the point of the inspection. Most people won't read a long report anyway, so why write it? Buyers generally want to get to the important information as soon as possible without having to read through a hundred or so pages. Pictures can be more powerful than words, so I would encourage you to add some photos of problems that you want to highlight for your customer. But overall, the report should be plain and simple, and get right to the facts.

SO YOU WANT TO BE A HOME INSPECTOR? HERE'S HOW!

I have provided a template of the inspection report I present to my clients with a cover page, a general information sheet, a real estate inspection report (which contains specific details about the property gathered during the inspection), and a building inspection contract. The book is organized around this template, and I will explain how to work your way through the inspection using this outline as you go through the book.

As a home inspector, it is important that you never leave any blanks in your report—it's best to cover yourself and the work you do by giving as much information as possible, as a problem could develop after your inspection or before a closing. In addition, if the house you are inspecting has furniture or any personal belongings inside, this could present a problem. A full inspection may not be possible, as these objects could make it difficult to see parts of the house. For example, there could be a hole in the wall or imperfections in the flooring that are covered by couches or rugs. In this case, simply mark "not fully visible" or "NFV" for short.

Happy home inspecting! My goal is to make this process less stressful for you.

General Information Sheet Overview

The General Information Sheet is on the first page of the Inspection Report and can be found in the back of this book. If you are doing an inspection for a realtor, include the listing agent's name, the buyer's agent's name, the seller's name, and the buyer's name. The next item would be property address. You will also need to include an access phone number, e-mail address, and any special notes, instructions and directions to the property. Be sure to write down any concerns that the buyer may have expressed about the property and address his or her concerns in the report. Last but not least, include the inspector's name (i.e., your name) and the date of the inspection.

As stated above, a blank inspection report is in the appendix of this book.

The following will help you fill out the report.

1.   Visual inspection ordered by: _____ (fill in the name, usually either the buyer or seller). Ask the seller the approximate

age of the home. You can also find it in local property records. Knowing the age of the home is an important part of
the inspection.

2. Building type: single-family, duplex, condominium, or other?

3. Is the property vacant or occupied? Who is there with you:
    the owner or tenant?

4. Weather conditions at the time of inspection: what is the out-
    door temperature? Is it clear, overcast, or rainy?

5. Persons at site: listing agent, buyer's agent, seller, buyer,
    others?

Insert the following note in your report:

> Note: This report contains technical information that
> may not be easily understood. A verbal consultation with
> the inspector is essential. The inspection company cannot
> be held liable for any uninformed interpretation of the
> report's contents. If you were not present during the in-
> spection or have any questions, please call the office for a
> verbal consultation or we will assume you have purchased
> the property in its current state.

> We suggest that clients ask sellers if any features of
> the property are shared in common with neighbors. Also,
> ask if there were any structural modifications made with-
> out permits or by an unlicensed contractor, and if there
> are any known zoning violations on the property. In the

report we may suggest a qualified contractor be called in to make any repairs, in which case we have completed our obligations and have no further liability.

6. Are the electricity, water, and heating on, off, or not applicable?

7. Is the house locked or otherwise secured? Yes or no, and by whom? Someone must lock up the house when you leave, and you must include this information in your report. This is important, as you do not want to be held responsible should someone else gain entry and damage the house.

8. Has the contract been signed and paid: yes or no?

9. To whom was the report given: buyer, buyer's agent, etc. (You should give the report to whoever hired you and paid for the report. It is up to him or her to give it to someone else, not you.)

10. Buyer paid $_____
    Seller paid $_____
    Check # _____

Real Estate Inspection Report

The real estate inspection report is the form that contains the findings from the inspection. It covers each section of the property, and following it will guarantee a full report and a satisfied client. The report is in sections containing subsections. For example the first section is "grounds" and the subsection to inspect is the "driveway" (which is just one area to inspect in the grounds section of the report). The real estate inspection report can be found in the back of this book. Take a minute to look over the template and become familiar with how it is laid out. Follow along while reading through each section to ensure filling it out fully.

Grounds (Where you will include information about the following):

- **Driveway:** Look for cracks in the driveway—these are trip hazards. Note its general condition. Examine the sidewalk leading to the house and note any cracks and hazards on your form. These are often overlooked, as the buyer is usually focused on the house itself and not the grounds. Look for any additional sidewalks or paths around the house, for example paths with stepping stones; check these to see if any are unstable.

- **Grading Landscape:** Check to see whether or not the yard drains away from or toward the house; the yard should always drain away from the house. Check the landscape for any tree limbs hanging over the house that may be too close or may be rotten and liable to fall onto the house. Limbs that are too close to the roof may damage the roof when wet and the wind blows. Note any large trees near the house whose roots may damage the foundation.

- **Retaining Walls:** Retaining walls are usually found on properties where the home has been built into the side of a hill. Their purpose is to hold back dirt and sod during heavy rain. Check the condition of any retaining walls and note this on your report. The retaining wall could be wood, concrete, or stone. Is it leaning, damaged, or rotten?

- **Patio and Patio Enclosures:** Check any screens carefully for tears or rips and look for screens that are old and fragile, or so flimsy they could be damaged by a strong wind that could rip it apart (put that on your report). If they seem fine at the time of inspection, note that on your report. Check to see that there are guide wires at the corners of the enclosure for stability. These are sometimes rusted, broken, or missing, and that should be noted on your report. The structure holding the screen should be sound and attached to the concrete patio. It may also be attached to the fascia of the home. The fascia is the flat board around the house that the shingles hang over and where most rain gutters are attached. Check that the fascia is in good condition. Also, check to see if the gutter needs to be cleaned (if it contains debris, such as leaves).

- **Front Porch:** The roof of the front porch will usually be held up by columns. Check for water stains or cracks on the porch ceiling. Check the base of the columns to see if they are in good condition or if they have been damaged by moisture. If they are painted, you will need a pointed object such as a knife or ice pick to test the base of the column. But they may not be entirely of wood. Builders sometimes place blocks of concrete or metal under the column, so they are less likely to rot. If the floor of the porch is concrete, note any cracks. If it has wood flooring, you should note any rotten boards.

- **Decks:** Check all decks for proper support and rotten boards. If you are not sure about the condition of the deck, note on your report that it should be inspected by a licensed contractor. Decks have fallen because of improper support, or having been built by an unlicensed contractor. Decks, especially elevated ones, can be hazardous if overloaded with furniture or people.

- **Exterior Stairs:** Stairs may be made of wood, metal, or concrete. Check wooden stairs carefully for water damage, weather damage, and rot. Pay attention to the handrails as well as the stair supports to make sure that everything is solid. Metal stairs can also be damaged and the metal is sometimes covered with concrete. In areas where winter snow is common, salt is often poured on the steps to melt the snow, which can also damage the metal. Note any areas of rust or deterioration. Sometimes rain will cause the same problems as snow and salt, and the supports will need to be repaired or replaced.

- **Fences and Gates:** Always note the condition of any fence and gate and the material of which they are made, which is usually wood, chain link, or PVC. Check that the gates are in good working order and have the proper hardware such as hinges, handles, and locks.

Exterior and Foundation

- **Walls:** Houses are built of various materials. Some are made with block, a wood frame with wood siding, or a wood frame with sheeting that can be covered with brick or stucco. Stucco is a plaster-like finish. If stucco, the stucco should be between three quarters and one inch thick. When a house is more than two or three years old, there will often be some settling cracks on the outside walls. These, and their size, should be documented. A crack wider than the width of a quarter (that is, one you can slip a quarter into) is cause for concern. Water can get in through these cracks, rot the wood, and attract termites. Small, superficial cracks are to be expected in older houses. These superficial cracks can look like the paint is dried and cracked. I have seen homes that one day have normal settling cracks the width of a quarter, and two days later they were a half inch wider. This scenario was not normal. You could check the house next door for evidence of settling cracks. If you find cracks there too, then the foundations may have been built in dirt that was not compacted. If the cracks are larger than the width of a quarter, the house may be on a sinkhole and a specialized sinkhole company should be called in for further investigation—note this on your report. If the house you are inspecting is a new home without carpeting and the slab (concrete floor) is exposed, check the concrete for any cracks. Big cracks suggest that the dirt or sand underneath the slab is not compacted; moisture (and even bugs) could enter the house through the cracks. You should also check records for the city and the surrounding area to see if sinkholes are common. For example, parts of Florida are riddled with sinkholes and a home buyer or seller should be aware of this.

- **Trim, Soffits, and Fascia:** While filling out this part of the inspection report, walk around the house and look for damage to any trim around the doors or windows. Check the soffits (which is the overhang of the roof on the outside of the house) and the fascia for rotten wood. Look for attic vents—openings for ventilation—which should be covered with screens, registers, or louvers to keep pesky wasps, bees, and other insects or bats from flying into the attic.

- **Chimney:** The chimney should be higher than the peak of the roof, otherwise it will probably not draw properly and the room will fill with smoke when a fire is lit in the firebox. Also look to see how the rain will run off the roof onto the side of the chimney; the chimney should be protected with good flashings. The flashing should be properly installed and high enough that water and snow will not get behind it. If the mortar in a brick chimney was mixed with too much sand, it will be a magnet for water to enter the structure and run down the face of the chimney inside of the house. If the chimney has a terra-cotta lining, it should go all the way up to the top of the chimney with no broken pieces. You can do this is by shining a flashlight up the chimney, which should give you enough light to see if the lining is in good shape. If the chimney is metal, make sure that all the sections are put together properly. You can also check a metal chimney with a flashlight, or look up for sunlight shining through improperly attached sections, but you may not always see that. If you're in any doubt about the chimney's condition, note on your report that the chimney should be checked out by a chimney sweep. If the chimney is used frequently, this is a good idea anyway because of the creosote that builds up inside the chimney. It can catch on fire and should be cleaned out regularly. Sometimes you will find that animals have made nests and in doing so dropped debris down the chimney. Every chimney should have a usable damper to close it off from the outside when not in use so as not to waste heat and air conditioning. Check that the metal lining or firebrick in the firebox is in good condition. Check to see if there is an ash dump to the outside—check that it is clear and can be used. If the fireplace has a gas starter, it is always best to ask the homeowner/seller to light it. In some cases you may have to do it; if you must light it yourself, be careful not to fill up the firebox with gas before striking a light, as this could result in an explosion and you could lose your hair, eyebrows, or worse! If you are uneasy about lighting the gas starter, note that it should be inspected by a fireplace contractor. (Take note: LP gas is more dangerous than natural gas, because it can build up faster and takes longer to disperse, but be very careful with both.)

- **Foundation:** This was touched on earlier in the inspection report, specifically in the wall section, because an unsound foundation will result in damaged walls. It is the foundation that prevents wall cracks, so you can get some idea of the foundation's condition by inspecting the walls. But the foundation in the crawl space or basement under a conventional house is different. In a home with a basement, check the walls for water intrusion. In a home with no basement, the foundations have pillars or columns underneath the house holding up floor joists. In older homes you'll find these pillars or columns on the sides of the house as well as under the house. They should sit on a concrete foundation and be made of something solid, not of wood and certainly not of a single log. The best are made of concrete pillars or blocks, or brick on concrete. Pillars in newer, conventional-type homes will have a piece of galvanized sheet metal on the top of the pillar. It will be turned down slightly, to keep wood-eating organisms from climbing up the pillar and eating the floor joists. In older homes this may not be the case. Check the floor joists to see if they are in good condition. Also note if there are any steel beams under the home. While you are under the house inspecting the foundation, always look for standing water or wet spots in the dirt. This could be a sign of a water leak from the house plumbing or it could be from a broken sewer line under the house. You will see any evidence of leaks in the sub-flooring and should note that in your report. In some homes the space between the outside columns will be bricked up and have holes for ventilation. These bricks don't provide any support for the house; they are there for appearance only and to keep large animals out.

- **Framing:** The framing is covered up with siding and Sheetrock. If you can see it bare, it will be much easier to inspect. It is important to note how straight the frame is; on occasion, you may see a wall that is bowed because the studs under the Sheetrock are not straight. If the carpenters had furred out the two-by-fours (by adding a strip of wood) before covering them with Sheetrock, this won't be noticeable.

- **Outside Hose Bibbs/Outside Hose Faucet:** The terms "hose bibb" and "hose faucet" are used interchangeably by professionals. They are located on the outside of homes, and they are used to attach a hose. Some plumbing codes require a vacuum breaker on the outside faucet to prevent water from being sucked back into the domestic water system. Problems can arise in the absence of vacuum breakers. For example, let's say someone leaves a hose running in a barrel in which car parts are soaking, making it caustic water, and there is a fire in the neighborhood at the same time. A fire truck can hook up to the fire plug, and then negative pressure in the system will draw water from the barrel into the domestic water system. When the fire is over and the water pressure is back to normal, this caustic water will still be running through the pipes and could cause illness. Vacuum breakers can be purchased at any hardware store and attached to the end of a faucet. Note on your report whether or not outdoor faucets have vacuum breakers. Check that the handles are in good condition and do not spray water around the pipe stem when they are turned on.

- **Roof/A Shingled Roof:** Roofs are often supposed to last twenty-five or thirty years but sometimes will only last twelve to sixteen years, depending on local weather conditions. Where the sun is intense, very bright, and hot, a roof will normally last about twelve to fourteen years. If the old shingles were not removed and a new roof was put over the old shingles, the life of the second roof is only approximately nine years. So the first thing you need to determine is whether this is one roof or whether a second roof has been added over the top. You can also ask the homeowner if he or she knows when the roof was installed. Most of the time, people will be honest and tell you the truth. Unfortunately there are some dishonest people out there, so you must be able to determine for yourself if the roof is really the age that the homeowner has told you. Look from the ground to see if the shingles are curling, missing, or torn. The most common shingled roof has three tabs and looks uniform. But in a dimensional or designer roof, the shingles are not in a uniform row. You can do a more thorough inspection by walking the roof to look for torn or missing shingles. But before you walk on any roof, you need to go into the attic to make sure that there is no rotten wood under the shingles. Sometimes there is a hole in the roof from a discarded air vent, and the roofer will shingle over the hole rather than patching it. While in the attic, look for daylight around all the vents protruding through the roof (such as plumbing vents); this could mean the flashings are not installed properly. You might not notice this from the outside and could fall through the patch. Some roofs—such as slate or tile, which are easily cracked or broken—are better to not walk on. If damaged, the seller might then want you to repair the roof. When you come across this type of roofing, it's better to do an inspection from underneath in the attic, in order to look for water stains. Bring along a set of binoculars so that you can put your ladder up against the house and view the roof through the binoculars. In any case, check the flashings around any vents protruding through the roof and around the chimney. The flashings around the vents need to be snug around the piping and, in some cases, wiped with roofing tar. Sometimes these flashings are lead and will have holes chewed in them by animals, which will cause a leak.

- **Roof Lines:** There are six basic roof shapes: gable, gambrel, mansard, hip, flat, and shed. All roofs need vents to let heat out of the attic. Heat and humidity trapped in an attic will allow mold to grow and everything in the attic will become mildewed.

- **Vents and Flashings:** Sometimes on a gabled roof there will be a vent at the top or end of the gable. In roofs with an overhang, there should be louvered vents around the house in the soffits. Louvered vents and soffits help keep the attic cooler by releasing the hot air from the attic.

- **Gutters and Downspouts:** Look out for gutters that are stopped up or have no downspouts. Downspouts should drain onto a splash block or driveway and should drain approximately two or three feet away from the house, so water doesn't undermine the foundation of the house.

- **Attic:** It is important to check the density of insulation in the attic. Most insulation will flatten out over time and sometimes will not even be as thick as the two-by-four rafters that the Sheetrock is nailed to. Put down in your report what type of insulation was installed: fiberglass, cellulose, rock wool, or some other type. Make sure to note on your report whether you think more insulation is needed. The rule of thumb is that there should be approximately six to eight inches of insulation.

Garage Area:

(As a reminder, be sure that you are following along with the blank inspection report included at the end of this book—it will make the explanations clearer and ensure a more thorough inspection.)

- **Roof:** If the garage is not attached to the house and the roof of the garage is different, note this on your report.

- **Floor:** Note the type of floor. Normally it is concrete.

- **Ventilation:** Note whether the garage area has windows or doors that can be opened for ventilation.

- **Service Door:** This is the side or back door to the garage. Make sure that it is in good working order and that there is no rot at the bottom. You should also check to see if the lock works properly.

- **Overhead Garage Door:** This needs a safety check. You do not want the door to come down on someone as he or she walks under it, or on the car as it's driving out. The best way to do a safety check is to hit the "close" switch and then put your arm or hand under the door as it comes down to see if it goes back up. You should do this at about waist high so that you can get your arm out if the door does not pass the safety check. If you put any type of pressure on the bottom of the door as it comes down, it should start moving up. Some garage doors are equipped with light beams (or laser beams) at the bottom of the doors, and if you obstruct the light beam, the door will move back up. You can check this by putting your foot through the light beam to enable the safety feature. Always note if the door comes down properly or if it makes a loud noise as it ascends or descends. It may need some oiling or minor repairs. Check the bottom of the garage door for any rot or deterioration.

- **Laundry Room:** If the washer and dryer are to be sold with the house, ask the buyer if they would like to have them checked. If so, run the washing machine and dryer through a full cycle to see if they are both in working order. Note whether the dryer is electric or gas.

- **Basement:** Some homes will have basements, and it is important to check to see if there are any watermarks on the walls from water intrusion. Some basements are prone to water intrusion and will have a sump pump in the basement. A sump pump is usually in a sunken area of the floor and water runs into the basin that the pump sits in. Once in the basin the water is pumped outside. You can check by pouring water into the sump pump to see if it is working properly.

Master Bedroom:

- **Doors:** Check the doors leading into the bedroom and bathroom and make note of the locks, if there are any, and if they are in working order.

- **Bedroom Windows:** These windows should be checked for a number of things. See if there are any breaks in the glass, if they open/lock, if they have screens, and if there is any wood rot or black mold around the frame. If there is mold or wood rot this could be an indication of water intrusion or window sweating. Some windows you will find are not made to be opened and do not have screens. These windows would be picture windows, stained glass windows, etc.

- **Bathroom Windows and Vents:** Always check bathrooms for windows and whether they open and lock. If there are no windows, check to see if there is a ceiling vent with a fan. All bathrooms need either windows that open or a ceiling vent with a fan to get fresh air into the room and to remove moisture from the room after a hot shower or bath. Without them, mildew can form in the bathroom. Be sure that the fan is working properly; some fans are on a separate switch and some are turned on by the light switch.

- **Electrical Outlets:** Most older homes will not have GFCI (Ground Fault Current Interruption or Interception) outlets. The GFCI breaks the circuit faster than the breaker in the main panel box, providing extra protection. For example, if you dropped a hair dryer into a sink filled with water, it would be important to have these GFCI outlets. GFCI outlets were not required in older homes, so you cannot note this as a defect unless it is a code violation in your state. However, do note on your report if the house does not have GFCIs. This protection can be added by the new buyer. As you go through the rooms, check each outlet to make sure that it is working, that the polarity is correct, and that the outlets are grounded. Reverse polarity in an outlet makes it easier for someone to be shocked, as the circuitry is reversed. Outlets in older homes may have only two prongs, in which case you will need an adapter on your tester to check to see if they have both a positive and negative. The main panels in older homes should be grounded even if the outlets are not.

- **Ceilings and Fans:** Check the fans to see if they are functioning properly. Ceiling fans can be operated with a remote, so make sure that the remote is present and working. Ceilings should be checked in every room as you go through the house. Look for any patches on the ceiling. Also look for discoloration that could be caused by a recent leak. In two-story homes, there can be a plumbing leak directly under bathrooms. Examine the ceilings closely around fireplaces for water stains and discoloration, because this could be a sign of bad flashings. (Flashings are described in the roof section.)

- **Floors:** As you go through the home, note the condition and type of flooring in every room, especially if the floor is tile—cracked and loose tiles could be an indication that the floor is settling. On the second floor of the home, walk around each room to see if the floor squeaks. Usually the second floor subflooring is plywood put down with nails. Over time, the nails will work themselves up and out, causing the subfloor to squeak as it is walked on. The subfloor very seldom squeaks if it is put down with screws. If the squeaking becomes annoying, the carpet may need to be taken up so screws can be put in the subfloor.

- **Smoke and Carbon Monoxide Detectors:** Be sure and check each room for smoke detectors and note on your inspection form where they are located and if they are in working order. Inform the people in the house before you test them so that you don't catch them off guard. Understand that some smoke detectors are connected to the alarm system; these should be tested by an alarm company. In that case, it would be best to write in your report that the detectors were "noted but not tested." Carbon monoxide detectors are especially important for homes with gas appliances or furnaces. If you see any sprinkler heads on the ceilings, make a note that they are there, but ask a sprinkler company to test the system.

- **Bedroom One:** Note the location of this bedroom and follow the same steps outlined above, checking the doors, windows, electrical outlets, ceiling and ceiling fans, floors and flooring, and smoke and carbon monoxide detectors for this and any additional bedrooms. Follow the same above steps for additional bedrooms: two, three, etc.

- **Bathrooms:** You will have bathroom number one (master), bathroom number two (guest), number three (powder room), number four, number five, etc. Be sure to specify the location of every bathroom in the house.

Master Bath:

- **Toilet:** First check to see that the seat is not broken, and look for cracks on the bowl inside and out and on the tank. Check the shutoff and the supply line to the tank for leaks. If no leaks are found, shake the bowl with your hands to see if it is loose on the floor: it should be tight. If it is not secure, note that on your report. Also note any leaks that you might have found. If you find that the toilet is loose, suggest that it be reset with a new wax ring, as it will allow sewer gas into the house if left improperly connected to the floor. (As a side note, my youngest daughter thought at one point she wanted to be a home inspector, so I brought her along on an inspection with me. I asked her to see if the toilet was loose on the floor. Of course, I only expected her to rock it from side to side. Instead she grabbed the toilet and lifted it up so high that I was shocked! I had to explain to her that you only rock it to make sure it was secured properly. She had the strength of a super hero that day, I suppose. You will want to gently rock the toilet. If the toilet is loose, rocking it will ensure that you don't break it.)

- **Sinks or Lavatories:** Sinks can also be called lavatories if they are found in the bathroom. Examine all sinks to see if any faucets are loose or leaking around the stems. If water appears around the faucet handles, then it is leaking around the stem. Check for drips after turning the faucet off. Look under each sink for leaks and check for water stains on the floor of the cabinet. You can check the drain by running your hand over the pipes, including the P-trap under the sink. While you run your hand over the pipes, look for moisture. The P-trap is the curved pipe under the sink. Every time water is drained from the sink, the P-trap keeps water trapped, which keeps sewer gas from coming into the house. Also check the sink for any cracking or rust. If you notice any imperfections in the sink, make sure to note that in your report.

- **Cabinets and Cabinet Doors:** It is always a good idea to check these areas and make note of their condition.

- **Electrical Outlets:** See if they have GFCIs. If not, make a note on your report. GFCI outlets should be used within six feet of any water fixture; note in your report whether these outlets are GFCI protected or not. Remember that the buyer may want to add them.

- **Ventilation:** If there are no windows in the bathroom, there should be an exhaust fan in the ceiling. This is not only meant for getting rid of odors, but also for removing moisture in the air to prevent mold developing from the steam of a hot shower or bath.

- **Tub:** Check the tub for any flaws, such as chips in the porcelain. If you can tell the difference between a steel, fiberglass, or cast-iron tub, note what type it is. If you do not know the differences, it would be a wise move to go to a plumbing supply house with a showroom and take a look at these types of tubs. After you see and touch them you should be able to identify them during your inspection. If you tap on a steel or cast-iron tub with your knuckle, you will be able to feel the difference. Check tubs to see if the stopper/pop-up/drain plug is working. Also check the caulking around the tub to see if the grout is in place or missing, and make note.

- **Shower:** Make sure that the showers have good grout and caulking around the trim. Faucets for the shower or tub should be examined for any leaks around the escutcheon—this is trim placed around the handles of the shower valve and around the shower arm at the wall to cover the holes that the shower handle or arm make coming through from the pipes. If the shower is tiled, it should be tested for moisture, which would suggest that the pan is leaking. For this you can use your two-pronged tester on walls adjacent to the shower. Focus it low near the floor to see if there is moisture in the Sheetrock or baseboard. If there is, further testing will be needed to see if the shower pan is leaking. This must be noted on your report and tested by a licensed plumbing contractor.

- **Floors:** Note the type of floor on your report: tile, carpet, wood, etc.

- **Shower door**: Make sure the door shuts properly and no water spills out on the floor. Be sure to check for missing grout. If any grout is missing, note it in your report.

    Note: Follow the same procedure for any additional bathrooms in your inspection report.

Living Room/Dining Room:

- **Doors:** Be sure to check any doors that lead to the living room/dining room. Make sure that the front door has weather stripping, trim, and working locks. Check to see if all outside doors open inward so that the hinges are on the inside of house.

- **Windows:** Check the windows to see if they open, are in good working condition, have any cracks, and have screens.

- **Electrical Outlets:** Check these in each room as described in the electrical section.

- **Ceilings and Fans:** Check these in every room and also check for ceiling stains.

- **Floors:** Check these in every room. Note the type of floor covering.

- **Fireplaces** (if applicable): if there is a fireplace, check it as explained earlier.

- **Interior Stairs:** Be sure and note if they are covered with carpet and need to be cleaned or replaced. Check the baseboards for any damage, and also see if they need any cleaning. Look to see if they have been chewed on by any animals. Check to see if they are painted and if there are any chips in the paint. Make sure that the handrails are not loose. It is most important that the handrails are sturdy.

Den/Family Room:

- Check the doors, windows, electrical outlets, ceiling, fans, floors, and fireplaces. Use the same procedures as used above for the living room/dining room.

Kitchen and Appliances:

- **Refrigerator:** It should be working at a minimum of forty-one degrees. Aim your temperature laser at an object that has been in there for a while, such as a milk carton or cold drink. Check the registered temperature; it should be forty-one degrees or less. The freezer compartment needs to be set below freezing. I tend to prefer anything from three degrees to twenty degrees, but this will vary depending on homeowner preferences.

- **Oven/Stove:** Always check to see if the eyes/burners turn on and if the clock is working. Set the oven to 250 degrees and use your temperature gauge, oven thermometer, or temperature gun to check if the desired temperature has been reached. Also check to see if the range and oven are attached to the wall or floor. A mounting stove is a safety feature for most new stoves to ensure that it will not tip over if any weight is put on the oven door. An unstable stove could be fatal; for example, children climbing on the oven door could knock a boiling pot of water over on themselves. Note on your report whether the stove is mounted to the wall or to the floor.

- **Dishwasher/Disposal:** Drains are normally connected to the disposal. The first thing you need to do is to make sure that the disposal is working and that the drain is not stopped up. Turn on the water and let it run in the disposal; if it doesn't back up, you can turn the disposal on. If you hear a noise in the disposal (a rattle, hum, or clanging), turn it off immediately—something may be stuck inside. As a home inspector, you don't need to free the disposal, simply report that it's jammed. Look down in the disposal with a flashlight and make sure that whatever is stuck inside the disposal can be easily removed. Always carry mechanical fingers. This tool has a push button feature where prongs open up and can help you grab any object in the disposal. This tool has been handy on my home inspections because I have pulled glass, pennies, and spoons out of the disposal before. It is up to you if you want to remove anything from the disposal so that you can check to see if it is working properly. After looking closely at the disposal, it is time to inspect the inside of the dishwasher. Make sure that it's clean and that there is nothing wrong with the gasket around the door. To ensure that the dishwasher is working properly, you should run it through a cycle while you are inspecting the rest of the house. Do not run the dishwasher if the sink line or disposal have a stoppage. Also check to make sure that it is anchored properly, either to the bottom of the countertop or the sides of the cabinets. This is important to prevent it from tilting or tipping over if someone opened the door and pulled the bottom tray out.

- **Kitchen Sink:** It's important to make sure that there are no leaks from the drain, and the best way to do that is to run hot water into the sink. Hot water will show leaks better than cold. Run your fingers over the P-trap in the pipes under the sink. Also check the shutoff valves to make sure that they're not dripping. You don't necessarily need to turn them off and on because that might start them leaking around the stems. Just make sure that they're not leaking at the time of inspection and look closely to make sure there's no water under the sink. There may be some water stains in the cabinet, which could be from water getting up on top of the sink and running under the faucet. You should also check the faucet for drips. Note any water stains in your report, and suggest that they be investigated further to identify the source of the problem.

- **Microwave:** Microwave wattages vary; some heat faster than others. All we are really interested in as home inspectors is checking to see that the appliance is working and not leaking radiation into the room. The best way to check this is to fill a small, glass, microwave-safe container with water. Place the container of water in the middle of the microwave and turn it on for about ten to fifteen seconds. After that time, check to see if the water is hot. Be careful touching the glass; you may need to use a hot pad to pick it up so that you do not burn your hands. If the water is hot, the microwave is working. Next, put a bigger glass of water in the microwave. Have your microwave meter ready and turn the microwave on. Run the meter slowly around the edge of the door to check for microwave leaks. Interestingly enough, nine out of ten microwaves leak. It is important to inform the homeowner of any leaks and especially which side of the microwave is leaking the worst so that they can avoid that side as much as possible while the microwave is in operation. This is even more important for people with pacemakers or anything similar, as they can be damaged by radiation. (That's why restaurants post warning signs: "microwave in use.")

- **Kitchen Floors:** Note the type of flooring in the kitchen and how many layers of floor there may be underneath. Sometimes people put ceramic tile or wood over the original flooring. The best way to check is to look in front of the dishwasher: if the flooring goes under the dishwasher, then that probably was the original flooring. If it does not go under the dishwasher, then the flooring was added on top of the older floor and might cause a problem if the dishwasher had to be replaced. Most dishwashers fit into an opening that is thirty-four inches high from the floor to the bottom of the countertop. Adding a floor, such as wood or tile, could reduce that by as much as an inch, making it hard to move the dishwasher out; the homeowner may have to cut the legs off the old dishwasher and try to find a new dishwasher with dimensions that fit. Make a note that this could be a problem.

Plumbing:

- **Main Lines:** The main line is the water service. In newer homes, this line is underground and normally comes up on the side of the house. This is where you will find a shutoff valve, a hose bibb, and a pressure blow off valve (these can also be called Apollo valves). In some areas where winter temperatures drop below freezing, these lines will run underground into the basement, and there are no exposed pipes on the side of the house. In these cases, there will be a shutoff valve in the basement or perhaps a valve that's called a "stop and waste." When these are shut off, the water will go into the ground, draining the pipes holding water inside the house, and will actually drain under the house. This happens in case there is no heat in the home; there will be less chance of the pipes freezing and bursting if there is no water in the pipes.

- **Supply Lines**: These lines run to the fixtures in the home. Supply lines can be of different types of piping, including galvanized steel, pex piping, cpvc, and copper. To find out what type of piping is used inside the house, check the connection near the water heater, which is usually the same piping as in the rest of the home. There are exceptions to this though; for example, when a water heater has been replaced, they may change it from copper to another type of pipe. If the connection is copper, then there is a good chance that the rest of the piping in the home is copper, especially if it is an electric water heater. If it is a gas water heater, the same rule can apply, but it must be a pipe that will not melt from heat (such as copper or steel). This is because the piping is close to the flue pipe, which is carrying hot exhaust to the outside.

- **Sewer Lines:** Sewer lines need to be checked to the best of your ability. You can flush and run water to see if there's any backup in the house; usually it will back up in the shower or tub first because that's the lowest fixture. If there are no issues with backups, then find the section on your report that says "sewer" and mark it OK at time of inspection. Walk around the house to look for clean-out plugs; note the location of any on your report. Clean-out plugs are useful when there is a stoppage; a plumber can remove the cap to the clean-out and insert his cable. Drain lines in the home are usually cast-iron, PVC, copper, or galvanized steel. In newer homes, galvanized steel is only used for waste arms, but PVC is also used for waste arms, drains, and sewers. The sewer outside the home can be made of terra-cotta tile, PVC, cast iron, concrete, or bituminous fiber pipe. (Bituminous fiber pipe is better known by the brand name Orangeburg. It was a popular pipe in the Second World War when cast iron was hard to come by. Bituminous fiber pipe is made of cardboard and tar.) Check to see how many plumbing vents are coming out of the roof. There should be at least one main vent of three- or four-inch pipe and perhaps smaller vents of one-and-a-half- or two-inch pipe in other locations in the roof, depending on local building codes and the age of the house. At the very least, you do need to determine if there are vents for the plumbing system. If there are none, check in the attic to see if perhaps they don't go through the roof. If that is the case, sewer gas could be moving into the attic. Note this in your report.

- **Fuel System**: The fuel system is for heating and cooking; in some cases you will find that the heating system is natural gas, LP gas, or heating oil. Make a note of this on your report. If none of these are present, it is an all-electric home. Be sure and check the water heater to see if it's gas or electric.

- **Water Heaters**: These can be either electric or gas. Codes vary on how they should be connected. The most important thing is to see if it is leaking and if it is working properly. Go to the furthest fixture from the heater, turn on the hot water, and let it run until the water gets hot. Then put a thermometer under the hot water and see what the temperature is. Federal and State regulations require that factories set water heaters at exactly 120 degrees Fahrenheit. If the water temperature is higher than that, note that on your report. The features that need to be inspected on the water heater are the shut-off valve and the temperature and pressure relief valve. The shut-off valve is for turning off the water should the heater develop a leak. The temperature and pressure relief valve come into play if the heater overheats. It should be pointed down to the floor, so that it will not spray on anyone, and it should have a pipe running from it, preferably extending two or three inches off the floor. In the rare case of overheating, this is a safety feature in case the controls went haywire. The heater may overheat and the water would turn to steam and cause it to blow up so that's a very important item to check. The need for the temperature and pressure relief valve allows the release of steam or water. If you can read the serial number or the model number, you might want to write that down for the buyer and also the gallon capacity. The manufacturing year is usually hidden in the serial number. Note any leaks on the piping and even the heater itself. Make sure to note if it is gas or electric. If it's gas, note the type of gas, LP or natural. If gas, the piping on the gas line should have gas cock or shut-off valve. Some municipalities require an expansion tank at the water heater, because water will expand when heated. This is called thermal expansion. Expansion tanks are required when there is a backflow device or a check valve in the water service. There is an exception when a pressure blow-off valve is installed on the water service.

Electrical and Air Conditioning:

The first thing you should note is whether an overhead or underground service is coming into the house.

- **Main Panel:** Write down what the amps are for the main panel, usually 100 to 250 amps. There should be a main breaker for the whole house that cuts off everything found in the panel. The total number of amps coming into the house will be written on the main breaker. The smaller breakers in the main panel box will also have amperage numbers on the switch. Check the other breakers to see how many of them are 110 volts and how many are 220 volts and write that on your report. Each single breaker will have an amperage number written on the breaker. All breakers are 110 volts, but if two are connected together, they are 220 volts. If you find breakers larger than 30 amps, they may be a 220-volt breaker.

- **Subpanels:** As you move through the house, look for subpanels. These are sometimes found near major appliances, such as water heaters. If you find any subpanels, just make sure to mention the location of them. If you don't find any, you can note N/A on your report. Check to see if the wiring in the house is aluminum or copper by removing the cover very carefully (because you don't want to be shocked), either at the main panel or the subpanels. (In my opinion, the main panel is the best option.) In past years there have been a lot of fires from aluminum wiring for 110 volts extending to outlets in the wall. Look at the breakers and see which have copper and which have aluminum wiring. The larger aluminum wiring is usually not a problem if it is 220 and goes to the air conditioning, clothes dryer, or electric range. Larger wiring doesn't expand and contract as much as smaller wiring. If you find small aluminum wiring going from 20- or 30-amp breakers, you must note that on your report because it is more likely to be a problem. Aluminum wiring should be noted on the report.

- **Outlets and Switches:** Check the outlets to see if they are in working order (we have covered this in the room-to-room inspection). You need to have a tester with three lights that will tell you if they are working, grounded, and have the correct polarity. Note any outlets with reverse polarity and where the grounds are not working.

- **Air Conditioning (A/C) Unit:** The air conditioning should be turned on immediately when you enter the house for the inspection so it has time to run. After turning the air conditioner on, note the brand name of the unit. See where the filter is and note if it can be changed easily. Check to see if there is currently a filter in place and if it is the correct size—if it's not the right size, then it's not filtering properly. (Filters should be changed every thirty days.) Check that it is put in correctly—a mark on the edge of the filter shows the direction of the airflow; the arrowhead should face the direction of the air return. Look inside the air handler to see if the coils in the fans are clean and note if it needs cleaning in your report. Also look at the registers where the air conditioning comes out to see if they have any dirt or mildew. Mildew (which might look like soot on a grill) is an indication that the ducts and registers need to be cleaned and sanitized. The A/C unit's compressor and condenser are located outside the house. While it's turned on, check to see if the fan is running. If the fan isn't running, it's not operating properly. Is the outside compressor surrounded by a lot of shrubbery? If so this can cut down on the airflow, and the shrubbery may need to be trimmed. Also look to see if the unit is full of grass or dirt because this will cut down on airflow through the fans and the condenser will need to be cleaned. Even though the A/C unit seems to be putting out cold air, it may not be working at its full capacity. Stand by the return air close to the air handler and use your temperature gun to check the temperature of the air there. Also test the temperature of the air coming out of the register in the rooms. There should be between twelve- and twenty-degrees difference between the return and supply. For example, if the supply line is at sixty-eight degrees coming into the room and the air going into the air handler is at eighty degrees, the difference is twelve degrees; therefore, the unit is working properly at the time of the inspection. If your findings are outside of this range, the A/C unit should be checked by an A/C company. (A word of caution: the word "mold" can scare some people in relation to their air conditioning, so I would suggest that you use the term "mildew.") If the A/C has mold, it can be cleaned by a company and sanitized in the duct and air handler. Some homes have window A/C units. The only thing you can do for these is check to see if they have a filter, if they are clean, and if the condensate is dripping outside away from the house. Turn them on and see if they cool the room. If not, then note that on your report.

- **Heating:** Heat pumps are used in some parts of the country. These heat pumps are essentially air conditioning units, but running in reverse for the heat. They should not be tested in certain weather conditions. For example, if the outside temperature is above 70 degrees Fahrenheit I would not turn on the heat to check the heat pump, as this could damage the compressor. Do a visual check and note that the heating system looks OK but was not inspected due to the outside temperature. Since the heat pump functions like the A/C, but in reverse, if the A/C works then the heat pump should be working fine too. If it's cool enough, say 65 degrees outside, you can turn the heat pump on by switching the thermostat to heat. But turn the system off first, and let it rest for about five or ten minutes before switching it to heat. Warm air should come from the registers soon after switching to heat. In colder areas of the country, heat pumps, if used, will need assistance heating the home in very cold weather. The homeowner can switch to emergency heat on the thermostat, and heat strips will kick in. If there is no heat pump and only air conditioning, you will find heat strips in the air handler. You may also come across a home with a gas furnace using the same ductwork that is used by the air conditioning. In that case, half of your air handler unit will be electric (the A/C) and the other half of the system will be gas (gas furnace). These can be fueled by natural gas, LP gas, or oil. Natural gas furnaces should be checked to see if they are burning properly. Make sure that there are no holes in the combustion chamber. Also look to see if the vent is extended properly. If the combustion chamber has a hole in it, the flame on the burners will be blown around. In other words, it will not be a steady flame because air is entering the chamber and keeping the flame from burning steadily in one spot. You can also check the chamber with mirrors and a flashlight to look for any cracks or holes. On a gas furnace, it should be vented with at least double wall pipe going through the roof with a proper vent cap.

Most codes state that there should be two-inch clearance around vent pipe when it passes through combustible material. Hot water or steam boilers for radiators or radiant heat should be checked by a licensed gas company that specializes in boiler installation and repairs. The only thing you can do is check to see if they turn on, heat, and turn off properly. If you cannot do those things, just note that the boiler and radiant heat should be checked by a licensed heating contractor. These systems can have many issues, such as leaks in the radiant heat under the floor, in the blow-off for the steam radiators, and in the condition of the boiler and burners. A lot of these boilers were converted from coal to gas. The boiler systems, if they are hot water systems, can be open-end or closed systems. Steam is always a closed-in system. In some areas, some homes are heated with oil, which has its own set of problems. It's best to confirm that the oil tank is safe and that the controls are working properly. These should be checked by a licensed heating contractor. Remember that you aren't there to make any repairs or to quote any codes. Your job is to find out whether things are in working order at the time of the inspection, so do not hesitate to turn it over to another professional if you have any doubts about the heating system.

- **Pool and Spa:** For a proper inspection the pool needs to be in operation. If it is not operating or so dirty that you cannot see the bottom, an inspection would be impossible. The first thing you need to do is look at the walls and the bottom of the pool. Is the pool above the ground or in the ground? Pools can be finished in concrete, marcite, vinyl, or fiberglass. Examine these surfaces for any imperfections, such as cracks or rough and discolored places in the fiberglass or concrete. If the finishing is cracked or rough it will need some repairs. Also look for missing tile—sometimes tile is installed around the edge of the pool at the waterline. This tile does not show dirt as much as the smooth surface of the pool's walls.

Make sure that the drain in the bottom of the pool is in place and is held down by screws. The best drain covers are dome-shaped on top; this shape helps prevent swimmers from getting tangled up in the drain. This type of drain is also recommended in spas. Check the filter at the scupper drain, where the water would exit the pool, and check that there is a basket inside the drain to catch leaves, debris, and unsuspecting small animals that swim in the pool. Open the top of the drain cautiously. I have found snakes and frogs before on an inspection, which surprised me when I wasn't prepared for them.

After that, move to the pump and filter. Make note of the type of filter in place. Some have a canister with a drop-in filter that can be replaced. Some are in a fiberglass or steel tank filled with rock and sand. Make sure that the pump is working. If the pump has a tag on it, you may be able to see the horsepower of the pump and if so, this should be included in the report. There should be a small filter at the pump with a basket inside to catch debris, like the scupper drain. This filter cannot be opened while the pool is running. Turn the system off, open the filter cover, and check that the filter is in place and that the basket is in good condition with a good rubber seal on the bottom of the cover.

Check the return jets in the pool to make sure that there are not a lot of air bubbles coming out of them. If there are a lot of bubbles, this means that air is getting into the circulation system from somewhere. In that case, the system needs to be checked by a pool contractor. But first, check the filter next to the pump as the lid may not be sealed properly and allows air in. Sometimes a little Vaseline on the rubber seal will stop the air from coming in. If not, the gasket must be replaced. This is a common place for air to be drawn into the system and can easily be done by the homeowner.

Also see if there is an electrical box near the pool equipment. It should have a timer so the homeowner can adjust the amount of time the pump runs during the day. In the winter, the water does not need as much circulation as it does in the summer, except in freezing weather when it should circulate constantly so it doesn't freeze. During warm weather, the pump will usually run for about eight hours a day. In the winter, if it's above freezing, six hours a day is sufficient. Also note if there is a fence around the pool or if the pool is caged for safety reasons. The fence gate or cage door should have locks to keep small children out of the pool area. It's also important to note the deck type, which can be wood, cool deck, pavers, or brick. Inspect for any cracks or hazards, such as bad boards. Check to see if the lights are working in the pool. Check any pool piping that is above ground for leaks. If the pool does not have enough water in it then there is a chance of underground leaks; this should be checked by a pool contractor.

If the home has a spa, check to see if it is connected to the pool. Spas sometimes use the same pump as the pool and usually are made of the same materials. If there is a separate spa, such as a hot tub, then ask if it is included in the sale of the property; if not, there is no need to inspect it. If yes, then check that it has been grounded properly. While a spa connected with the pool may or may not have its own controls, hot tubs should have separate controls. The inspection of a hot tub spa, if present, is similar to the pool inspection: check the filters, jets, and lights. Run the hot tub or spa through all of its speed cycles. Check that it heats the water. If the heater has been turned off for some time, note in your report that it was not inspected for that reason. Hot tubs should have a removable cover to minimize heat loss. If there is no cover, note that in your report: without a cover the hot tub will be heated constantly, the pump will work harder, and the electricity bill will be unnecessarily high.

Overall Condition and Property Repairs:

- Once you have inspected the Pool/Spa (if applicable), you have almost reached the end of the report, but before we end, there should be a section to account for the overall condition of the house and a spot to summarize any property repairs that were touched on during the in-depth inspection of the house. The inspection report that I have included in the back of this book (the one you have been following along with) includes these sections and can be found on the last page of the real estate inspection report.

While you have made comments on different aspects of the home throughout the report, in these last pages you can draw attention to any concerns you may have, explain why tests weren't done, or summarize any remaining questions for your client. For example, there is no area on the report to note a problem with mold, but if you suspect a problem with mold in the house, you can note it in this section. Just write something like "probable mold, recommend further testing."

Remember, if you have any doubts about something, include it in the report and suggest further investigation by the appropriate contractor. The inspector's job is to point out problems, not to fix them. I have also included an inspection contract, which is located in the appendix with the real estate inspection report.

Conclusion

Included in the following pages are: a list of tools to bring with you to an inspection, a sample contract, a real estate inspection report, and pictures of rooflines as further guidance. These are the items that were given to me to implement in my inspections or as a guide. I hope it gives you an idea into how you would like to format your contract and inspection report as well. As a home inspector, you should have a contract before you do any work. Make sure to have your own attorney review your contract. Other templates are also available online if these do not suit your needs. In addition, your state or municipality may require you to get a license or a certification before going into the home inspection business.

Congratulations! You now have all the information you need to do a complete and sound home inspection on your own. I wish you all the best in your future inspections! Thank you for taking the time to read this book.

Tools to make your home inspection easier:

1. Small glass and hot pad to check that the microwave heats properly. Fill the glass with water and start the microwave. The hot pad is for picking up the glass and protecting you from burns.
2. Microwave leakage detector.
3. Laser temperature gun or oven monitor to check the oven temperature.
4. Two-pronged moisture meter to check for moisture in wood or Sheetrock.
5. There is also a moisture meter that can be placed on the walls. This does not have prongs and has a flat surface.
6. Binoculars to check roofs.
7. Three-prong electrical tester to determine whether outlets are operating correctly, are grounded, and have correct polarity, and to check that GFCIs are working properly.
8. Two-prong adaptor for the three-prong tester for older homes that do not have three prong outlets.
9. Compass to note which way the home faces.

10. Three mirrors of different sizes to check things that are difficult to get to, or a mirror on a long handle to check inside combustion chambers.
11. Screw-on gauge to check the pressure of the water system by screwing it onto an outside hose faucet and turning the faucet on: it should be thirty to sixty-five psi.
12. Stud finder to locate the studs in the walls.
13. Circuit Alert Pen to determine if a wire is carrying electricity (such "hot" wires should not be touched).
14. Electric screwdriver to remove the cover on the electrical panel.
15. Small and medium-sized flashlights and a large, powerful light for looking under the house.
16. First Aid Kit.
17. Mechanical Fingers to pick up items in hard-to-reach, dangerous, or unsanitary areas.
18. Miscellaneous items that can be useful: change of clothes or coveralls, gloves, kneepads, paper towels, toilet paper, aspirin or other pain killer, hat, sunscreen, and hand sanitizer.

SO YOU WANT TO BE A HOME INSPECTOR? HERE'S HOW!

COMPANY NAME
ADDRESS
ADDRESS

VOICE: FAX:
E-MAIL: WEBSITE:

BUILDING INSPECTION CONTRACT

Contract made between _____ (client), and COMPANY NAME

RECITALS

WHEREAS Client desires to have a visual inspection of the building located at:

_____

WHEREAS Inspector agrees to perform a visual inspection for Client under the terms and conditions set forth in this contract. In consideration of the mutual promises set forth in this contract, Client and Inspector agree and covenant as follows:

SCOPE OF INSPECTION

Inspector shall perform a visual inspection of open, accessible, and apparent building components, which are specifically identified in the "Inspector's Report." Inspector shall perform the inspection in a safe, skillful, and generally workmanlike manner in accordance with industry standards. Inspector shall in no event alter, build, repair, maintain, and/or service any building component, which falls within the scope of this contract. Upon the tender of delivery of the "Inspector's Report," inspector shall have fully and completely discharged the inspector's duty of performance under this contract.

PAYMENT

Client agrees to pay inspector the total sum of: **$**_____ for the visual inspection to be performed under this contract.

LIABILITY

INSPECTOR'S LIABILITY FOR ANY MISTAKE, OR OMISSION, WHICH ARISES WITHIN THE CLIENT-INSPECTOR RELATIONSHIP, ESTABLISHED BY THIS CONTRACT SHALL BE LIMITED TO A REFUND OF THE FEE PAID FOR THE VISUAL INSPECTION AND "INSPECTOR'S REPORT."

Client agrees to assume all risk of loss, which exceeds the fee paid for the visual inspection and "Inspector's Report" and to hold inspector, its officers, agents, and employees, harmless from and against any and all liabilities, demands, claims, suits, losses, damages, causes of action, fines or judgments, including costs, attorney's and witnesses' fees, and expenses incident thereto, for injuries to persons and for loss of, damage to, or destruction of property arising out of or in connection with this contract unless caused by the gross negligence or willful misconduct of inspector, its officers, agents, or employees.

SETTLEMENT AND WAIVER OF POTENTIAL CLAIMS

Client agrees to immediately accept a refund of the fee paid for the visual inspection and "Inspector's Report" as full settlement of any and all claims, which may ever arise out of or in connection with this contract. Wherein inspector tenders a full refund, Client hereby voluntarily agrees to waive all claims for damage or defects, which may develop or become visible at any time subsequent to Inspector's visual inspection.

DISCLAIMER OF WARRANTIES

Inspector makes no warranties or guarentees with respect to building, which is the subject of this contract. Any representations or warranties not included within this contractual writing whether expressed or implied, are hereby disclaimed. There is no warranty whatsoever on major or minor damages or defects, which may develop or become visible at any time subsequent to Inspector's visual inspection.

HAZARDOUS SUBSTANCES EXPRESSLY EXCLUDED

Hazardous substances are expressly excluded from the terms of this building inspection contract. Hazardous substances include, but are not limited to the following: odors, radon, pesticides, fungicides, toxins, carcinogens, all electromagnetic fields, and formaldehyde.

NO THIRD PARTY BENEFICIARIES

Client and Inspector understand, acknowledge, and agree that the "Inspector's Report" is intended for the sole use and benefit of Client. Client and Inspector desire no third party beneficiaries to this building inspection contract.

In Witness Whereof the parties have executed this building inspection contract this _____ day of _____.

_____   _____

_____
CLIENT   **AUTHORIZED AGENT**
and/or INSPECTOR

COMPANY NAME

ADDRESS (STREET)

ADDRESS (CITY, STATE, ZIP)

COMPANY PHONE / FAX

REAL ESTATE INSPECTION REPORT

CLIENT:

CLIENT #:

General Information/Notation:

NFV = not fully visible

X = OK at time of inspection

N/A = not applicable

SO YOU WANT TO BE A HOME INSPECTOR? HERE'S HOW!

GENERAL INFORMATION SHEET OVERVIEW

Buyer:_____   Buyer's Agent:_____

Seller:_____   Seller's Agent:_____

Property Address:_____

_____

Access Phone #_____   Cell #_____

Inspector:_____

Date:_____   Approximate Age of Home_____

1. Visual Inspection ordered by:_____

2. Building Type :
   ☐ Single Family   ☐ Duplex

   ☐ Condo   ☐ Other

3. Occupancy:
   ☐ Vacant   ☐ Occupied

   ☐ Owner   ☐ Tenants

4. Weather conditions:_____ F°   Dwelling faces_____

   ☐ Clear   ☐ Overcast   ☐ Rain

5. Person at Site:
   ☐ Seller   ☐ Seller's Agent   ☐ Other

   ☐ Buyer   ☐ Buyer's Agent

6. Utilities: ☐ On   ☐ Off   ☐ N/A

7. House Locked / Secured   ☐ Yes   ☐ No   By whom:_____

8. Contract Signed and Paid   ☐ Yes   ·   ☐ No   By whom:_____

9. Report Given to whom:_____

REAL ESTATE INSPECTION REPORT

SECTION: GROUNDS / EXTERIOR / GARAGE

GROUNDS   COMMENTS

DRIVEWAY	
SIDEWALK / PATHS	
GRADING / LANDSCAPE	
RETAINING WALLS	
PATIO ENCLOSURE	
DECKS	
EXTERIOR STAIRS	
FENCES / GATES	
ADDITIONAL COMMENTS	

EXTERIOR / FOUNDATION

WALLS	
TRIM, SOFFITS, FASCIA	
CHIMNEY	
FOUNDATION	
FRAMING	
CARPORTS / AWNINGS	
HOSE BIBBS	
ADDITIONAL COMMENTS	

ROOF

ROOFING TYPE / MATERIAL	
VENTS / FLASHINGS	
GUTTERS / DOWNSPOUTS	
ATTICS	
ADDITIONAL COMMENTS	

GARAGE

ROOF TYPE / MATERIAL	
FLOOR	
VENTILATION	
SERVICE DOOR	
OVERHEAD DOOR	
LAUNDRY ROOM	
BASEMENT	
ADDITIONAL COMMENTS	

SO YOU WANT TO BE A HOME INSPECTOR? HERE'S HOW!

SECTION: BEDROOMS / BATHROOMS

MASTER BEDROOM: COMMENTS

DOORS	
WINDOWS	
ELECTRICAL OUTLETS	
CEILING / FANS	
FLOORS	
FIREPLACES	
SMOKE DETECTORS	
ADDITIONAL COMMENTS	

BEDROOM #1 — LOCATION _____

DOORS	
WINDOWS	
ELECTRICAL OUTLETS	
CEILING / FANS	
FLOORS	
FIREPLACES	
SMOKE DETECTORS	
ADDITIONAL COMMENTS	

BEDROOM #2 — LOCATION _____

DOORS	
WINDOWS	
ELECTRICAL OUTLETS	
CEILING / FANS	
FLOORS	
FIREPLACES	
SMOKE DETECTORS	
ADDITIONAL COMMENTS	

BEDROOM #3 — LOCATION _____

DOORS	
WINDOWS	
ELECTRICAL OUTLETS	
CEILING / FANS	
FLOORS	
FIREPLACES	
SMOKE DETECTORS	
ADDITIONAL COMMENTS	

SECTION: BEDROOMS / BATHROOMS

BEDROOM #4 — LOCATION_____   COMMENTS

DOORS	
WINDOWS	
ELECTRICAL OUTLETS	
CEILING / FANS	
FLOORS	
FIREPLACES	
SMOKE DETECTORS	
ADDITIONAL COMMENTS	

BATHROOMS (#1, #2, #3…)

TOILETS	
SINKS	
FAUCETS	
DRAINS	
COUNTERS / CABINETS	
ELECTRICAL OUTLETS	
VENTILATION	
TUB	
SHOWER	
FLOOR	
ADDITIONAL COMMENTS	

MASTER BATH

TOILETS	
SINKS	
FAUCETS	
DRAINS	
COUNTERS / CABINETS	
ELECTRICAL OUTLETS	
VENTILATION	
TUB	
SHOWER	
FLOOR	
ADDITIONAL COMMENTS	

SO YOU WANT TO BE A HOME INSPECTOR? HERE'S HOW!

SECTION: INTERIOR
LIVING ROOM / DINING   COMMENTS

DOORS	
WINDOWS	
ELECTRICAL OUTLETS	
CEILINGS / FANS	
FLOORS	
FIREPLACE	
SMOKE DETECTOR	

DEN / FAMILY ROOM

DOORS	
WINDOWS	
ELECTRICAL OUTLETS	
CEILINGS / FANS	
FLOORS	
FIREPLACE	
SMOKE DETECTOR	

KITCHEN / APPLIANCES

REFRIGERATOR	
RANGE	
DISHWASHER	
GARBAGE DISPOSAL	
KITCHEN SINK	
MICROWAVE	
DOORS	
WINDOWS	
CEILINGS / FANS	
ELECTRICAL OUTLETS	
FLOORS	

ALBERT E. WISE II

SECTION: PLUMBING / ELECTRICAL / AIR / HEATING

PLUMBING   COMMENTS

MAIN LINES	
SUPPLY LINES	
SEWER LINES	
FUEL SYSTEM	
WATER HEATERS	

ELECTRICAL

SERVICE	
MAIN PANELS	
SUB PANELS	
OUTLETS / SWITCHES	

AIR CONDITIONING

GENERAL COMMENTS	

HEATING

GENERAL COMMENTS	
VENTING	

SECTION: POOL / SPA

TYPE	
POOL / SPA FINISH	
DECKING TYPE	
FILTERS AND PUMPS	
ELECTRICAL	
PLUMBING	

NOTE:

IF HEATING SYSTEM WAS NOT INSPECTED, IT WAS DUE TO THE OUTSIDE TEMPERATURE BEING TOO HIGH. THE HEAT PUMP COULD NOT BE FULLY TESTED IN THE HEATING MODE WITHOUT POSSIBLE DAMAGE TO THE COMPRESSOR. HOWEVER, THE OPERATION OF THE HEATING AND COOLING CYCLES ARE IDENTICAL EXCEPT FOR THE DIRECTION OF THE REFRIGERANT FLOW. THE PERFORMANCE OF THE SYSTEM IN HEATING MODE IS THEREFORE USUALLY THE SAME WHEN COOLING. AN AIR CONDITIONING CONTRACTOR SHOULD BE CONTACTED IF HEATING IS DESIRED.

SO YOU WANT TO BE A HOME INSPECTOR? HERE'S HOW!

OVERALL CONDITION OF THE HOUSE

☐	ABOVE AVERAGE
☐	TYPICAL
☐	BELOW AVERAGE
☐	NEEDS NORMAL YEARLY PREVENTATIVE MAINTENANCE
☐	NEEDS CONTRACTOR / ENGINEER TO FURTHER EVALUATE / REPAIR
☐	NEEDS FURTHER TESTING TO DETERMINE IF MAJOR REPAIR(S) ARE NEEDED
☐	HAS MANY INACCESSIBLE, CONCEALED, FURNISHED, OR HIDDEN AREAS

PROPERTY REPAIR SUMMARY

ITEMS MARKED HERE AS NEEDING VISIBLE MAJOR REPAIR MAY HAVE A HIGH PROBABILITY OF INVOLVING A SIGNIFICANT EXPENSE AND/OR ARE VISIBLE FHA/HUD , HEALTH, SAFETY, OR PROPERTY PRESERVATION REQUIREMENTS — PLEASE CALL A CONTRACTOR TO MAKE REQUIRED REPAIR(S).

NOTE: MOST COMPONENTS OF HOMES ARE FUNCTIONAL (WORKING) BUT VIRTUALLY ALL OF THEM MAY/WILL NEED SOME MINOR REPAIR(S) OR ONGOING MAINTENANCE, OR COULD BE IMPROVED. THE INDIVIDUAL SECTIONS MAY HAVE MARKS THAT ASK YOU TO CALL A CONTRACTOR OR ENGINEER PRIOR TO CLOSE — IF NOT, CONSIDER THEM TO BE RECOMMENDATIONS AND NOT REQUIREMENTS.

THE FOLLOWING ITEMS SHOULD BE REVIEWED BY A LICENSED CONTRACTOR

_____
_____
_____
_____
_____

PROPERTY REPAIRS NEEDED

_____
_____
_____
_____
_____

NOTE:

If you have any questions, please call for verbal consultation.

If you do not call for verbal consultaion, we will assume you have purchased the property as is.

Ask the seller:

• If any features of the property are shared in common
• If any structural changes have been made without permits and if there are any known zoning violations

Inspectors are not responsible to report on:

1. Code Violations
2. Life expectancy of any items
3. Presence of pests (insects, rodents, or wood damaging)

Inspectors are not responsible to:

1. Provide estimates or warranties of any kind.
2. Report on the life expectancy, strength, or efficiency of any system or component.
3. Remove personal items or debris that obstruct visibility. Client is responsible for any risk/condition from areas inspector did not have access to during time of inspection.
4. Predict future conditions.
5. Provide results from tests or inspection not specifically contracted for.

BASIC ROOF SHAPES

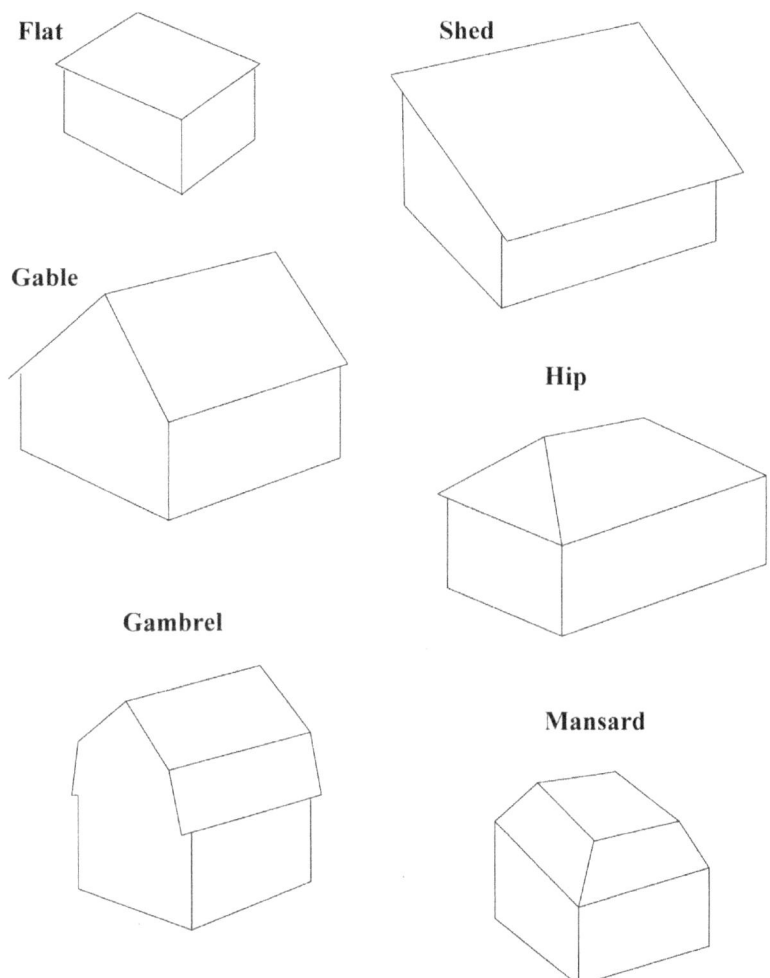

Flat

Shed

Gable

Hip

Gambrel

Mansard

www.ingramcontent.com/pod-product-compliance
Lightning Source LLC
Chambersburg PA
CBHW071816170526
45167CB00003B/1334